This book is dedicated with eternal love to Joseph Lyons - a wonderful son, brother and friend - in his memory and legacy to help the many that need mental health and well-being assistance and support within educational settings and their communities.

- *The Family of Joe Lyons and Trustees of Joe's Buddy Line*

For all the wonderful children I have worked with who continue to inspire me with their kindness, insight and courage.

Tina Rae

With thoughts always to Will, Alex and your families - thank you for inspiring the characters that will help so many. Your smiles and memories live on. For Will, Ben, Max & Emmy.

- *Dani Saveker*

Grateful acknowledgement and thanks are given to Tina Rae and Dani Saveker who have provided their services to produce the BUDDIES TALK book, entirely free of any payment and without requiring future royalties. All profits from the BUDDIES TALK book will be given directly to Joe's Buddy Line Charity. This generosity will help to continue and expand the much needed charitable work of Joe's Buddy Line Charity in providing a wide range of mental health and wellbeing initiatives to assist and support students and others within school communities.

ISBN: 978-1-7385799-9-0

BUDDIES TALK

MOVING FROM PRIMARY TO SECONDARY EDUCATION

WRITTEN BY **TINA RAE** DESIGNED & ILLUSTRATED BY **DANI SAVEKER**

FOREWORD BY **ROMAN KEMP**

Registered Charity Number 1193127

CONTENTS

Foreword from Roman Kemp	01
An Introduction	02
For teachers, parents and carers	03
Using Your Book	04
What's Included	05
The Buddies	06
Your Buddy character	07-10
1 Making Your Transition Work For You	11-14
2 Understanding Your Feelings	15-18
3 Anxiety and When To Ask For Help	19-22
4 Knowing That Feelings Are Not Facts	23-26
5 Developing Your Mind	27-30
6 Building Your Plan To Relax	31-34
7 Valuing Your Body and What It Can Do	35-38
8 Coping with Tests and Exams	39-42
9 Bullying – Why and What To Do	43-46
10 Creating a Positive Self-care Plan	

11 Creating A Calm-down Tool Kit	47-50
12 Learning To Control Your Mind	51-54
13 Using Kindness and Gratitude	55-58
14 Using Your Worries Well	59-62
15 Staying Safe – Including online	63-66
16 Creating Your own 'Buddies' Plan	67-70
Meet The People Behind The Book	71
About Joe's Buddy Line	72
Useful Resources and Support	73-75
Copyright And other Important Information	76
Index	77
My Progress Sheet	78

A foreword from our Buddy, Roman Kemp

Hi, my name's Roman and I'm a Trustee of the charity Joe's Buddy Line. I am passionate about the importance of being able to talk about what goes on in our heads. Finding ways to look after our mental health - just as we would for our physical health - needs to start much earlier than secondary school, and there's no better time than now. Sometimes, this means we need to have tough or difficult conversations, but that's okay - it's really important and brave to talk about how you feel.

This book - which I love, by the way - is a great place to start. Just like the Buddies, it doesn't matter what you look like, who you are, what's going on in your life, how many friends you have, if you're good at sport or not, or how good you are at your times tables; we all have good days and we all have bad days. We all worry about being good enough, fitting in and being liked. So, if we all worry about these things, perhaps we can start to talk together about this stuff, because then things don't feel as bad.

I talk for a living - on podcasts, telly and radio, but my favourite conversations are with my friends, family and the people I trust. If this book helps just one person to talk - you - then what an amazing thing that is!

In 2020, I committed to supporting big changes for positive mental health, especially in young people. It's about teaching kids how to start talking and equipping them with the tools needed to deal with the challenges we all face. I believe that the amazing world of the Buddies is transformational and much needed. It's about making it normal, and fun, to talk about feelings as well as being able to spot when other people need a helping hand. Looking out for your mates is something that needs to start in schools from a much earlier age.

And to the school family, teachers, parents and carers...this includes you too. Talking is just as important for adults - so welcome to the world of the Buddies!

Roman

BUDDIES TALK
MOVING FROM PRIMARY TO SECONDARY EDUCATION

Hello and welcome to The Wonderful World of the Buddies! This book is designed just for you, and we really hope that it helps you as you move from your primary school to your secondary school.

Moving to secondary school can be really exciting. There's lots to look forward to, but we can also worry about lots of things when we start a new school. You might have all sorts of questions in your head - for example, "Will I still be with my friends?", "What happens if I don't feel happy?", "What if I forget my homework?" and many more.

Everyone can feel worried and anxious. This is normal. There will be times when we find it difficult to manage and find that we need some extra help. There will be other times when we feel excited and happy to be doing new things and don't feel worried at all.

The most important thing is that **we keep talking**. Don't bottle up your feelings or worries. There are people who you can talk to and who can help you. Just like the Buddies, your friends probably have similar worries and excitement to you, so you can be a good buddy to each other - helping one another and sharing ideas and ways of coping.

So, let's get started together and work our way through this book. You will find lots of different scenarios to read and also some ideas that you can think about, talk through, and share with others. You will also be introduced to all sorts of little creatures; you'll meet Joe, Will, Poppy and many more Buddies. They will talk about their feelings and try to help each other find the best ways of coping. Hopefully, you will be able to learn some new ideas from them and they will inspire you to come up with some of your own tools and strategies!

An idea for you is to consider starting a journal or notebook as you work your way through the book. You can jot down any ideas or questions that you have or anything that you find out that may be new or helpful. Take your time and enjoy this book!

for teachers, parents and carers

This book is designed to help young people talk about difficult emotions, including those associated with times of stress and heightened anxiety.

The importance of expressing how we feel about things can't be underestimated. Being able to talk about how you feel can be very cathartic and immediately reduce our levels of stress. Sometimes just being heard by someone else can help us to feel more seen and ultimately, better understood.

For many young people, not being able to talk about how they feel can put them at risk of more significant mental health difficulties - both in their teenage years and in later life. This book is designed to engage children and young people in the process of becoming listening partners. In order to do this, they first have to acknowledge their own feelings and understand the importance of sharing those with others who may be able to help and support them.

This means understanding at the outset, that talking about how we feel is not self-centred or selfish. Talking about how we feel should also not be something that we stigmatise. If we have uncomfortable feelings and don't express them then we will simply hold them in our bodies, and this may cause trauma later in life - as stated previously.

What we need to be able to do is recognise, articulate, and express our feelings. A key message here is the fact that no feelings are unimportant. If we feel stressed, anxious, angry, upset, frustrated, or embarrassed, these feelings are very real and should never be dismissed. Many children and young people will have heard the unhelpful message that it is not okay to talk about these issues. They may have been told that they will get over it, they need to 'man up' or stop making a fuss. It is simply untrue and very damaging.

This publication is designed to support children and young people. To help develop their emotional literacy, the skills of recognising their feelings and those of other people, their ability to challenge ineffective thinking and to make use of a range of self-regulation strategies and well-being techniques which can become part of their everyday routines and ensure that they maintain overall well-being and good mental health. In engaging in this process, they will also be encouraged to act as well-being buddies for their own circle of friends and to share their own skills, developing the empathy and compassion that is needed to build and maintain mutually beneficial and positive relationships.

USING YOUR BOOK

There's no right way or wrong way to use this book - use it however you want.

Start wherever you want - dip in and dip out. You don't have to work through in order.

You can read, work through the tools in the 'playtime' section, talk with friends about the topics...and so much more.

Together, we will explore **16 specific topics**. Each one has been written to help and support the move from primary to secondary education.

To help, we will visit each topic through the world - and adventures - of **'the Buddies'**: a wonderful group of colourful little creatures. You can meet them all on page 5!

...and you can record your journey through the book by filling in the **"My Progress Sheet"** on page 78.

WHAT'S INCLUDED

16 Themed Chapters:

Each chapter is based on a scenario involving some of the Buddies. The theme is explored through the characters and how they try and help each other. Each interaction also provides a question for young people to think - and talk about.

To help with the theme being looked at, each chapter also provides a set of activities / tools to work through within the 'playtime' section. Within the chapter, you will find a link to access downloadable resources to support the activities and provide guidance and ideas.

Each chapter also includes a set of **Buddy Facts** and finishes with a quick check-in with Tiny Alf.

At the back of the book, you'll find a '**My Progress Sheet**' to colour in as each chapter is completed - regardless of what order they are done.

THE BUDDIES

Joe 	Will 	Poppy 	Tiny Alf 	Alex 
David 	Connie 	Annie 	Jamal 	Kono 
Theo 	Zach 	Manu 	Ella 	Anya 
Arti 	Zahra 	Rosie 	Mo 	Nageen 
Miss Hughes	Mr Stephenson	Dr Hussain	Mrs Hanson	Ms Jones

YOUR BUDDY CHARACTER

This is your personal 'buddy card'. Draw yourself as a 'buddy character'.

THE BUDDIES

My name:

About me:

My birthday:
My hobbies:
My height:
Any pets:
My favourite lessons:
My special qualities:
I like to be called:

What colour will you be?

Add your name

Add your character information.

06

# LET'S GET STARTED...MAKING YOUR TRANSITION WORK FOR YOU

1 MAKING YOUR TRANSITION WORK FOR YOU: PLAYTIME

01

STOP, THINK & REFLECT
Here are a few things to think and reflect about...

- ☐ Feeling nervous
- ☐ The first day
- ☐ Having homework
- ☐ Making new friends
- ☐ The school uniform

THE 'WHAT IF...?' GAME
Let's think about some 'what if?...' questions. What ideas can you suggest to answer each one?

What if...I get bullied?
What if...I don't make friends?
What if...I say the wrong thing?
What if...I can't find my classroom?
What if...I don't like my teacher?

03

COPING WITH CHANGE
Working in small groups, let's come up with some ideas to cope well with...

- ☐ The first day
- ☐ Travelling to school
- ☐ Doing homework
- ☐ Making new friends

Write down a few coping strategies - things you can use - to help.

02

GAIN A STAR AS YOU TRAVEL AROUND THE BOARD AND FINISH EACH TASK - COLOUR IT IN WHEN COMPLETED

05

CHECK-IN WITH TINY 'A.L.F':

One ACTION you can take:

What did you LEARN?

How are you FEELING?

INFORMATION CARDS

Now let's create a card with information you'd like your new teachers to know about you.

Here is an example:

- My name is Andrew Smith
- I'm very shy.
- I struggle to speak up in class.
- I prefer to work on my own.
- I manage better when I work directly with one adult.

04

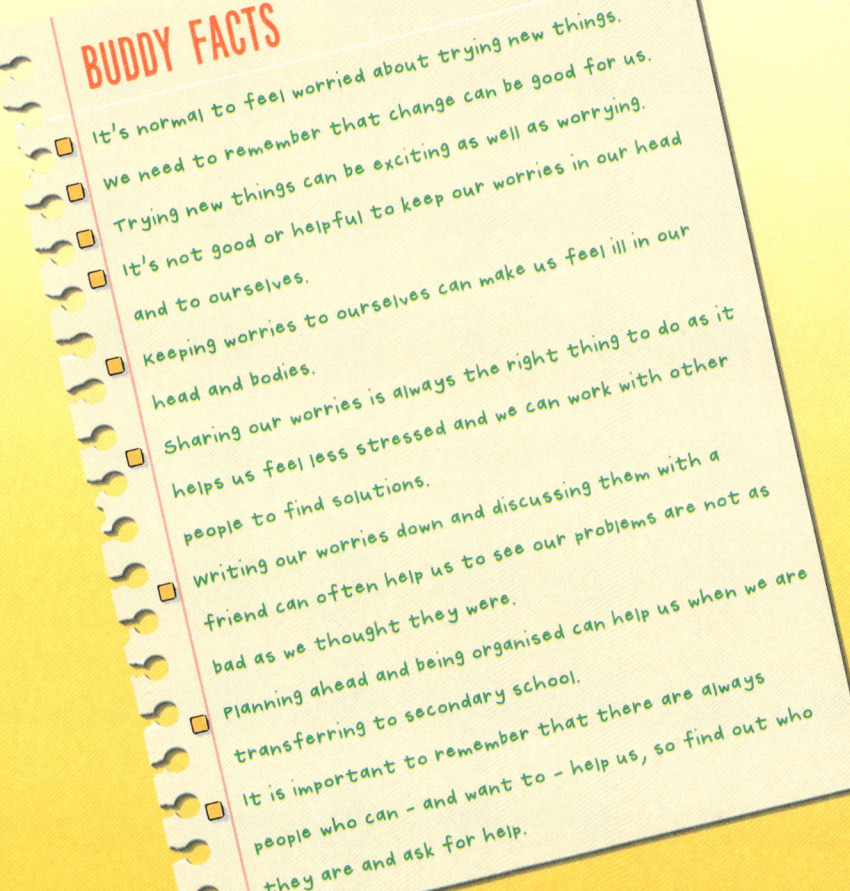

BUDDY FACTS

- It's normal to feel worried about trying new things.
- We need to remember that change can be good for us.
- Trying new things can be exciting as well as worrying.
- It's not good or helpful to keep our worries in our head and to ourselves.
- Keeping worries to ourselves can make us feel ill in our head and bodies.
- Sharing our worries is always the right thing to do as it helps us feel less stressed and we can work with other people to find solutions.
- Writing our worries down and discussing them with a friend can often help us to see our problems are not as bad as we thought they were.
- Planning ahead and being organised can help us when we are transferring to secondary school.
- It is important to remember that there are always people who can – and want to – help us, so find out who they are and ask for help.

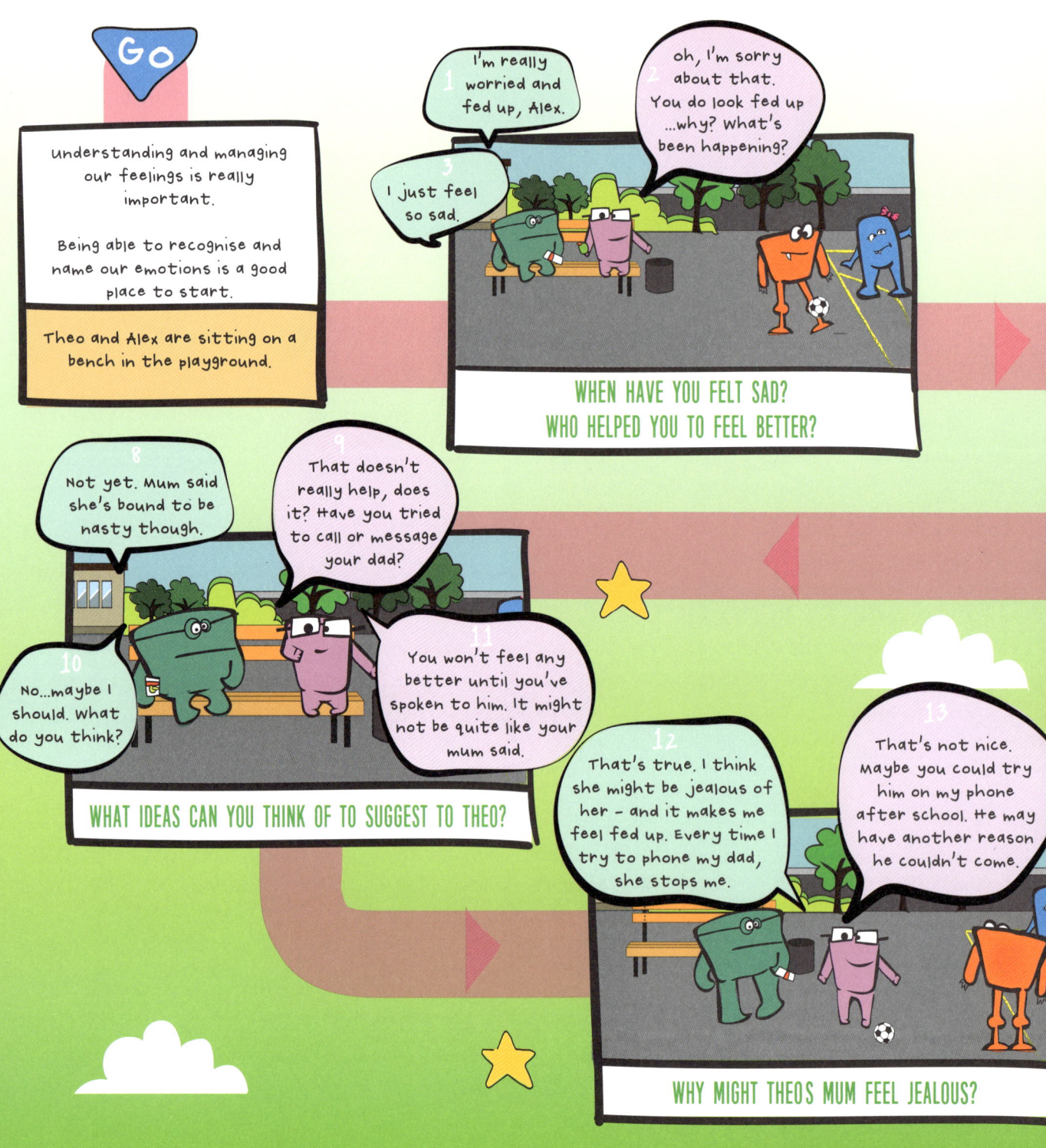

2 UNDERSTANDING YOUR FEELINGS: PLAYTIME

01

EMOTION CHARADES
Write a range of emotion words on pieces of paper. Put them in a hat. Take turns to pick a word and act it out – without speaking. The other players guess what emotion you're acting out

FEELING TEMPERATURE
Draw a thermometer. Write 10 at the top and -10 at the bottom. Zero in the middle

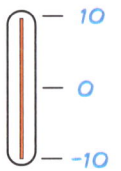

Mark where you are. When are you closer to 10? When are you at the lower end near -10

02

VISUAL EMOTIONS
Create a visual piece that shows your emotions – you can draw, paint, use blocks or cut a magazine up to create a collage.

03

13 GAIN A STAR AS YOU TRAVEL AROUND THE BOARD AND FINISH EACH TASK – COLOUR IT IN WHEN COMPLETED

04

FEELINGS STORM

In a 10 minute brain-storm, how many feelings can you name? Think of all the good ones and the bad ones... write down as many as possible.

EMOTIONS

BUDDY FACTS

- Understanding our feelings is very important. It helps us to begin to express how we feel so that others can understand us better.
- Understanding our feelings can also help us to recognise them in other people.
- There are no such things as 'bad' feelings. All feelings are valuable.
- We can have comfortable feelings such as happiness, gratitude and joy. We can have uncomfortable feelings such as anger, fear and sadness. Some situations can cause us to experience a mixture of both types.
- Everyone can get better at talking about their feelings and learn to manage the more uncomfortable ones. It takes effort and practice.

05

CHECK-IN WITH TINY 'A.L.F':

ONE **ACTION** YOU CAN TAKE:

WHAT DID YOU **LEARN**?

HOW ARE YOU **FEELING**?

TEMPLATES AND INSTRUCTIONS ARE AVAILABLE TO DOWNLOAD VIA: JOESBUDDYLINE.ORG/BUDDIESTOOLS

3 ANXIETY AND WHEN TO ASK FOR HELP

Anxiety is something we can experience when we are feeling overwhelmed.

It's normal to feel anxious from time to time.

Joe and Poppy are in the canteen having their lunch. Poppy isn't eating her food.

1. What's wrong Poppy? Why aren't you eating your food? I thought you liked pasta?

2. I do normally, but I don't feel hungry today – and haven't for the past few days.

3. You have to eat. My mum said it's really important to eat lunch.

4. I know Joe. I'm not doing it on purpose. I just feel sick and my tummy churns over.

CAN YOU DESCRIBE WHAT IT FEELS LIKE TO BE ANXIOUS? WHAT HELPED YOU TO FEEL BETTER?

11. She'd still want to know – and she'll see you're not eating, and that you're anxious. You need to talk about it.

12. You're right Joe. I'll try and talk to her.

WHO ELSE COULD POPPY TALK TO FOR HELP?

13. Do you promise me, Poppy? I'll message you tonight to check you've spoken to your mum.

14. Thanks Joe. That's a deal.

HOW DO YOU THINK POPPY FEELS NOW?

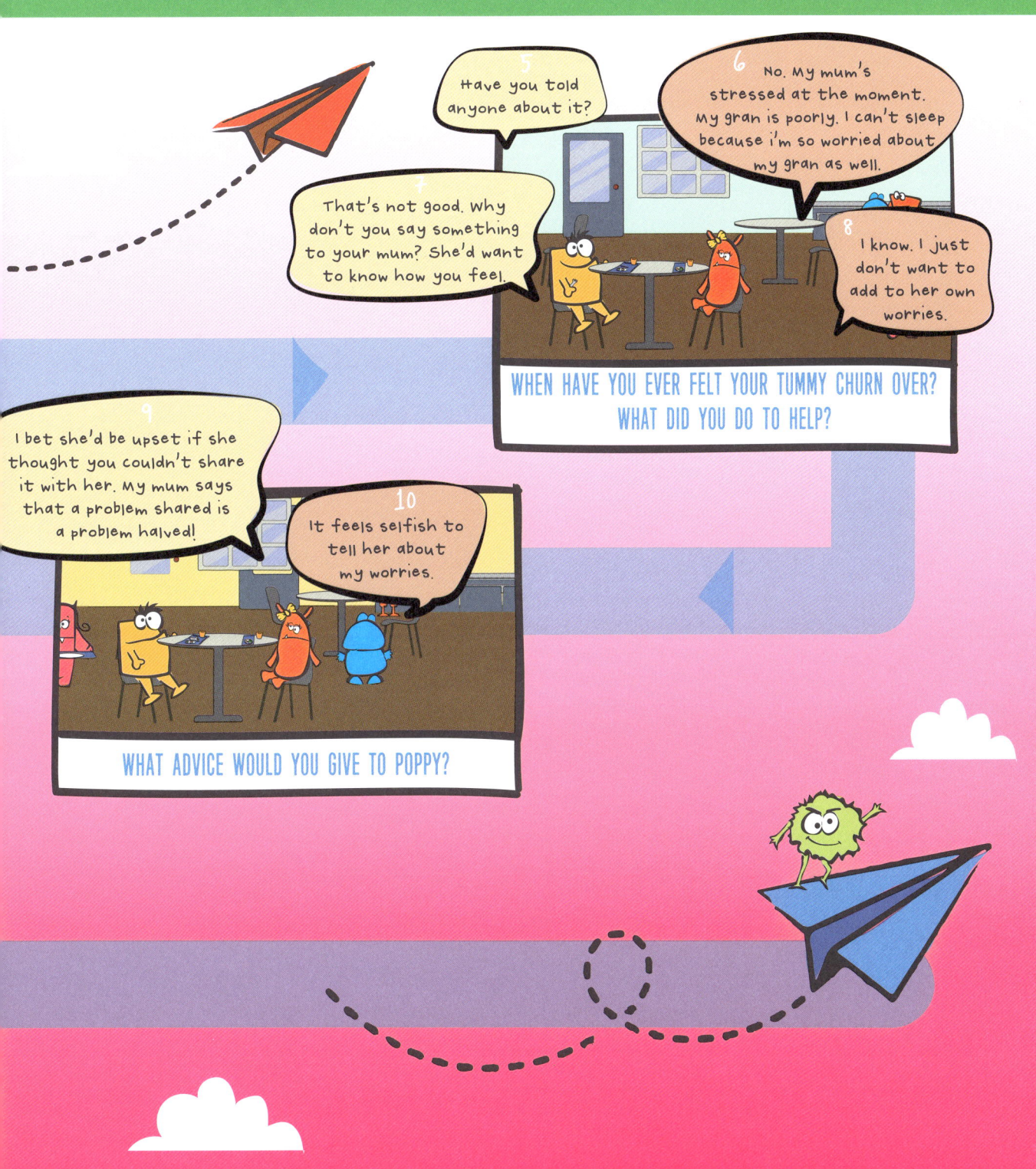

3 ANXIETY AND WHEN TO ASK FOR HELP: PLAYTIME

01

BREATHING MOMENTS
Find somewhere comfortable to sit. Focus on your breathing. When a thought pops into your head, accept it - and then let it float away on a cloud or like a leaf on a river. Think about each short breath you take - in and out.

GET CREATIVE
Doing a creative thing can help manage how you feel. Here are a few ideas....

DRAW
PAINT
DOODLE
SING
DANCE
COLOUR
READ FICTION

02

POSITIVE PICTURE
When you feel anxious, see if you can picture something positive and peaceful in your mind.
Close your eyes and think about your positive picture.

03

GAIN A STAR AS YOU TRAVEL AROUND THE BOARD AND FINISH EACH TASK - COLOUR IT IN WHEN COMPLETED

04

AN ACT OF KINDNESS

Doing something for someone else can help us to feel better.

Write a thank you note.
Tell someone what you admire about them.
Read to your little sister.
Pick up litter.
Hold a door open for someone.

BUDDY FACTS

- Anxiety can be thought of as the body's warning signal and is a normal response to a possible or real threat.
- It can help us in terms of preparing our bodies for action by releasing the hormone called 'adrenaline' – which provides the energy we might need to respond.
- This is vital when we need to escape from a difficult situation, but over time, a high level of anxiety can become harmful – particularly when it starts to interfere with our ability to cope with the stresses and strains of everyday life.
- It is important to always seek help when you are feeling overwhelmed by anxiety. Don't wait – you can talk about it and help to get it sorted!

05

CHECK-IN WITH TINY 'A.L.F':

ONE **ACTION** YOU CAN TAKE:
_____

WHAT DID YOU **LEARN**?
_____

HOW ARE YOU **FEELING**?

4 KNOWING THAT FEELINGS ARE NOT FACTS

Sometimes we can get caught up in a negative pattern of thinking. This can include thinking badly about ourselves, our situations and even our friends and family.

We need to remember that these thoughts create feelings that are not facts. We need to be able to question our thinking and feelings.

Annie and Connie are sitting in the hall during the head teacher's assembly.

They are trying to hide the fact that they are chatting.

9 It's okay. I know you're worried about it. But I don't think you're looking at the facts.

10 I'm so scared of messing up. At night I lie in bed imagining it all going horribly wrong.

11 But look at the facts. You've done the practice and your run-throughs are great.

12 My mind's running away with me! I need to think more positively.

HAVE YOU EVER FELT LIKE CONNIE?

13 I get it. When that thought is in your head say "I'm not thinking that" - think about all the times you did it right. Why would it be different now?

WHEN HAVE YOU THOUGHT NEGATIVELY? HOW DID YOU TURN THESE INTO POSITIVE THOUGHTS?

4 KNOWING THAT FEELINGS ARE NOT FACTS: PLAYTIME

01

TEST YOUR THINKING
Follow the steps...

Identify a negative thought.
What is the evidence for this?
What's the evidence against it?
What would your best friend say about the thought?
What would you say to your friend if it was their thought?
How true do you think the thought is now?

PMA
"Positive mental attitude" is a process we need to practice and strengthen. Think about these examples and how you can THINK, FEEL and DO with a positive mental attitude...

GETTING LOST IN A BUILDING
LOSING YOUR MOBILE PHONE
DON'T DO WELL ON A TEST
FORGET YOUR PE KIT

02

T.F.D. TRIANGLE
There is a cycle with our internal thoughts that we need to be aware of...

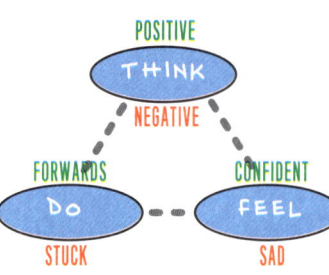

03

21   GAIN A STAR AS YOU TRAVEL AROUND THE BOARD AND FINISH EACH TASK - COLOUR IT IN WHEN COMPLETED

BUDDY FACTS

- ☐ The cycle of negative thinking, feeling and doing is a pattern that we can all get trapped in.
- ☑ Negative thoughts are thoughts that are pessimistic, distorted, or irrational. They can trigger stress, anxiety or depression.
- ☑ Negative feelings come from negative thoughts and can lead to feeling sad, lonely, angry or anxious.
- ☑ Negative behaviours come from our negative feelings and can lead to avoiding friends and family, shouting at people or hurting yourself.
- ☑ Negative behaviours can reinforce negative thoughts which reinforce negative feelings…it's a cycle – but one we can break
- ☑ Remember – we can all make 'thinking errors', but with action and help we can go to a better 'thinking place'!

CONTROL YOUR THOUGHTS

FACTS — think about the actual facts

↓

SOLUTIONS — what is possible based on the facts?

↓

STRATEGIES — ideas include: write it down, talk, describe it, and worry box

CHECK-IN WITH TINY 'A.L.F':

ONE **ACTION** YOU CAN TAKE:

_____

WHAT DID YOU **LEARN**?

_____

HOW ARE YOU **FEELING**?

TEMPLATES AND INSTRUCTIONS ARE AVAILABLE TO DOWNLOAD VIA: JOESBUDDYLINE.ORG/BUDDIESTOOLS

5 DEVELOPING YOUR MIND

A developing mind is when you believe that your abilities, intelligence and performance can be developed and improved.

People that develop their minds are more likely to take on challenges and learn from their mistakes. Sometimes this is called a 'growth mindset'.

Joe and Annie are sitting in the reading corner together. Annie is reading to Joe

1 Keep trying, you'll get there. So, it begins with...

2 I don't know what this word is, Joe. I'm trying to work it out in my head, but it won't come.

3 C and L.

WHEN HAVE YOU STRUGGLED WITH SOMETHING? WHAT HELPED YOU WITH THIS?

9 Look, we're all at different levels - we have different skills and talents.

10 I can't help it - everyone else finds it easy. It makes me feel sick and stupid. I can't read like you.

11 You'll be able to. Take your time and break the word down... Look "cl-an-des-tine"

12 I really want to be able to read well. What am I going to do when we go to secondary school? I might not be able to read as well as everyone else.

WHAT WOULD YOU LIKE TO ACHIEVE?

WHAT GETS IN THE WAY OF YOU ACHIEVING THINGS? WHAT HAVE YOU DONE TO GET PAST THIS?

 DEVELOPING YOUR MIND: PLAYTIME

01

KIND SELF-TALK

Practice talking to yourself in your head in a kind way. Here's an example...

UNKIND		KIND
I'm not good enough	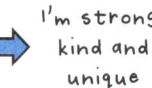	I'm strong, kind and unique

02

KIND THOUGHTS SCROLLS

Design and make your personal scroll full of kind thoughts about yourself.

Use your favourite colours. Keep it somewhere you can see.

03

BUILD A VISION BOARD

Using pictures and words, create a 'board' with your goals, hopes and dreams.

Include the things you most want in your life, the things you want to do and achieve as well as the feelings you want to have e.g excitement, calm.

GAIN A STAR AS YOU TRAVEL AROUND THE BOARD AND FINISH EACH TASK - COLOUR IT IN WHEN COMPLETED

CHECK-IN WITH TINY 'A.L.F':

ONE ACTION YOU CAN TAKE:

WHAT DID YOU LEARN?

HOW ARE YOU FEELING?

MY A.C.T PLAN

To help manage your emotions, well-being and how you feel about yourself, list things you can do for A.C.T:

ACTION
e.g running, swimming, singing

CALM
e.g breathe, sit outdoors, relax

THINK
e.g practice self-kind thoughts

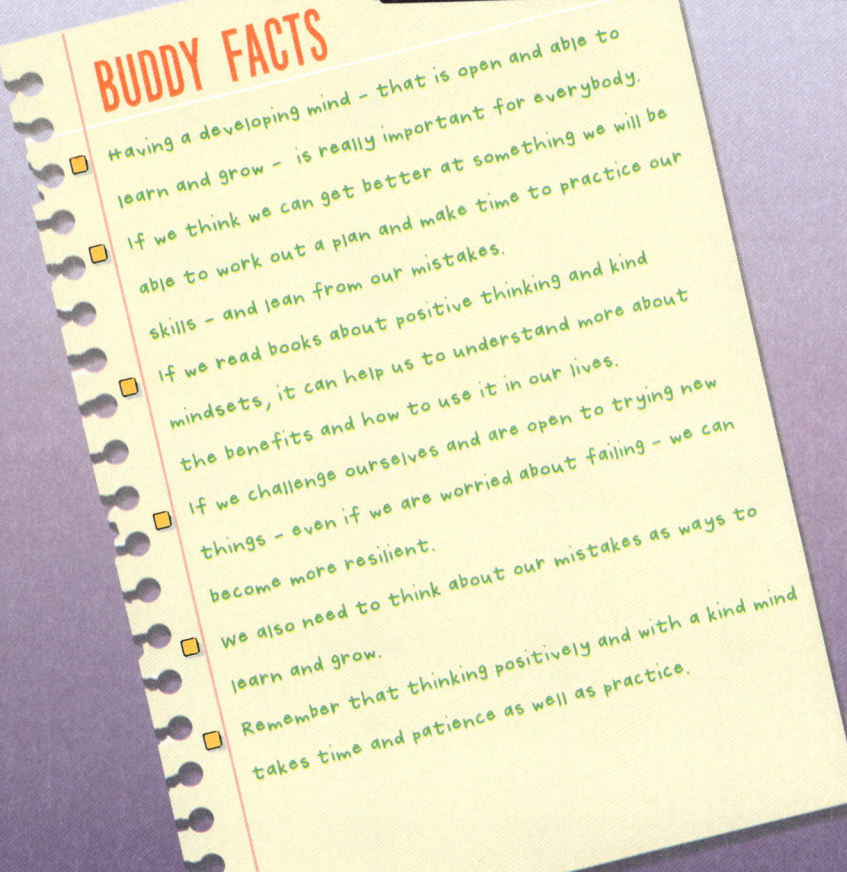

BUDDY FACTS

- Having a developing mind — that is open and able to learn and grow — is really important for everybody.
- If we think we can get better at something we will be able to work out a plan and make time to practice our skills — and lean from our mistakes.
- If we read books about positive thinking and kind mindsets, it can help us to understand more about the benefits and how to use it in our lives.
- If we challenge ourselves and are open to trying new things — even if we are worried about failing — we can become more resilient.
- We also need to think about our mistakes as ways to learn and grow.
- Remember that thinking positively and with a kind mind takes time and patience as well as practice.

TEMPLATES AND INSTRUCTIONS ARE AVAILABLE TO DOWNLOAD VIA: JOESBUDDYLINE.ORG/BUDDIESTOOLS

6 BUILDING YOUR PLAN TO RELAX

Relaxation is important for us all. Feeling tense and anxious prevents us being focused.

When we are relaxed our bodies release endorphins - natural chemicals to help us feel happy.

Alex and Zahra are running around the hall throwing beanbags to each other in their P.E lesson.

1 oh sorry! I dropped it. I keep doing it - I feel so tense.

2 It's just a game Zahra. Don't worry about it!

HOW DOES IT FEEL WHEN YOU'RE TENSE? HAVE YOU DEVELOPED WAYS TO REDUCE THIS?

7 It's just really hard. I feel like my parents expect me to be the best. I can't just go home and relax. They want me to do extra work.

8 So you mean you're doing even more work homework at night? Don't you have any time to watch TV or read ...or play?

9 Not really. It's making me feel so tired.

10 Have you told your mum and dad?

HOW DO YOU LIKE TO RELAX?

11 No. I just don't want to disappoint them. They are both good at everything and I don't want them to feel like they have a stupid daughter.

12 You know, I bet they would be so upset if they heard what you just said. You nee to tell them how you feel.

HOW MIGHT SOMEONE FEEL IF THEY AREN'T VERY GOOD AT SOMETHING?

 BUILDING YOUR PLAN TO RELAX: PLAYTIME

01

MY PEACEFUL PLACE

Relax and let your mind think of a special place – somewhere you feel safe, peaceful and calm.

When the picture is clear in your mind, describe it – using words and pictures.

RELAXATION DIARY

Over the next few weeks, if you can record your relaxation practice so you build better control.

Day/date:	
Relaxation score before: (10 is fully relaxed)	
Relaxation completed:	
Relax score after: (10 is fully relaxed)	

02

BODY RELAXER

Tense each part of your body. Hold for 5–10 seconds. Now relax them. Count to 100.

Keep practicing this. You have control over your body.

03

GAIN A STAR AS YOU TRAVEL AROUND THE BOARD AND FINISH EACH TASK – COLOUR IT IN WHEN COMPLETED

04

CALM ART

Creating art, colouring and painting can be helpful strategies to calm your mind.

Can you draw a 'calm and relaxed' piece of art? You can cut magazines, draw and colour. What do you think are relaxing shapes and colours?

BUDDY FACTS

- Relaxation helps release endorphins; a natural chemical that makes you feel happy.
- Relaxation can help muscles and calm your nervous system.
- Relaxation can help calm and clear your mind.
- Relaxation can sharpen your concentration.
- Relaxation can help your memory retention.
- Relaxation can decrease your mental tension.
- Relaxation can help promote your positive thinking.
- Relaxation helps reduce stress and anxiety in all humans.

05

CHECK-IN WITH TINY 'A.L.F:

ONE **ACTION** YOU CAN TAKE:

WHAT DID YOU **LEARN**?

HOW ARE YOU **FEELING**?

TEMPLATES AND INSTRUCTIONS ARE AVAILABLE TO DOWNLOAD VIA: JOESBUDDYLINE.ORG/BUDDIESTOOLS

7 VALUING YOUR BODY AND WHAT IT CAN DO

GO

Body image is how you think and feel about your body. It includes the picture you have in your mind, which might or might not match your body's actual shape and size.

Connie and Annie are standing in front of a mirror trying on clothes for their end of year prom.

1. What do you think Annie? Do you like this dress on me?

2. You look really nice in it. The colour suits you and you look slim.

3. I feel good in this one. I'm not worried about looking slim – it doesn't matter, does it?

4. Well of course it doesn't matter to you. You always look slim so there's no need for you to worry.

HOW DO YOU FEEL ABOUT HOW YOU LOOK?

7. Oh yes, I forgot about that! That's why it doesn't fit anymore. I just thought I was getting fat!

8. But you've got lots of lovely dresses. I don't think you've put on weight. You've got taller! After all, you're nearly 12 now and you got that green dress when you were 10!

DO YOU THINK APPEARANCE TELLS US EVERYTHING ABOUT WHO A PERSON IS?

7 VALUING YOUR BODY AND WHAT IT CAN DO: PLAYTIME

MY AMAZING BODY

My amazing hands help me to...

My amazing mouth allows me to...

My amazing feet help me to...

My amazing voice means i can...

My amazing face is special because...

MY BODY CAN...

what does your body do for you in terms of living healthy and happy life? Let's think about eating, dancing, breathing, sleeping, walking, lifting... Draw yourself and label what each thing does for you.

 02

03

MY HEALTHY BODY

write a list of all the things that help to make your mind and body healthy.

GAIN A STAR AS YOU TRAVEL AROUND THE BOARD AND FINISH EACH TASK - COLOUR IT IN WHEN COMPLETED

04

I'M UNIQUE...

Just like the 'Buddies', we are all unique.

Draw yourself - as a Buddy character if you want - and write all of the special characteristics and qualities you have that other people can't see or wouldn't know from looking at you.

BUDDY FACTS

- It's important that we value our bodies and treat them with respect. We need to look after them in the right way.
- We need to make sure we have a good diet and take regular exercise as well as avoiding drugs and other harmful substances that can damage us physically and mentally.
- Poor body image can be very damaging. Some children do not feel happy with their bodies simply because they are comparing unreal images that they see in the media and online.
- Children and young people are more at risk of developing a poor body image during their adolescence. This is due to a range of different factors, but with the right support they can overcome this.
- The most important thing is when you feel dissatisfied or embarrassed about your body, you talk to someone you trust and that can help you.

05

CHECK-IN WITH TINY 'A.L.F':

ONE **ACTION** YOU CAN TAKE:

_____

WHAT DID YOU **LEARN**?

_____

HOW ARE YOU **FEELING**?

_____

TEMPLATES AND INSTRUCTIONS ARE AVAILABLE TO DOWNLOAD VIA: JOESBUDDYLINE.ORG/BUDDIESTOOLS

8 COPING WITH TESTS AND EXAMS

We can all become anxious, worried, and stressed when we have to take any test or exam. It is normal to feel like this and we shouldn't be ashamed if we experience these feelings.

It is so important to ask for help.

Joe and Arti are sitting on a bench overlooking the football pitch. Joe looks sad.

1. What's going on Joe? You seem down. What's happened?

2. Nothing, I'm fine - really.

3. You don't look fine to me!

4. I'm fine, honestly. Don't push me on this.

WHAT ARE THE SIGNS OF SOMEONE BEING WORRIED?

13. Have you talked to them?

14. Course not - I'd make them worry. They'd just go over the top and get more anxious about me - which would make me feel even worse.

15. Why don't you just try and say that you're worried about them worrying about you. May be if they thought you didn't want them to get upset on your behalf. What do you think?

16. I'm not sure - I don't want to make things worse.

WHO COULD YOU TALK TO?

17. I don't think you could make it worse by just telling them that you're worried and feel under pressure from them. It's how you do it that matters.

18. Okay, what would you suggest Arti? How would you do it? You seem to be much better at this than me.

WHAT COULD JOE SAY TO HIS PARENTS?

35

COPING WITH TESTS AND EXAMS: PLAYTIME

01

5 CALM STEPS
1. Breathe deeply for a few seconds
2. Water – take a drink
3. Pause – take a moment
4. Think – happy thoughts
5. Visualise – a good outcome

EXAM TIPS
Arrive on time and prepared.

Plan your approach and timing.

Allow more time where there are higher marks.

Read questions carefully.

Check the instructions.

Stay focused on what you're doing

02

PLAN & PREPARE
Exams can be stressful so plan ahead...

- Identify the source of stress
- Prepare what you can do
- Create your script to say in your head
- Strategies to keep stress down
- Re-evaluate – what worked and didn't work

03

GAIN A STAR AS YOU TRAVEL AROUND THE BOARD AND FINISH EACH TASK - COLOUR IT IN WHEN COMPLETED

BUDDY FACTS

- ☐ It's normal to feel anxious when faced with exams and tests.
- ☐ Never feel that you are the only person who is experiencing stress. Stress can be positive as it can increase levels of concentration, but only if we manage it effectively.
- ☐ We can all develop strategies to manage stress, but this takes practice – it doesn't happen on its own.
- ☐ We can all use strategies on a daily basis to keep calm.
- ☐ We can also all use strategies to manage when we first get into the exam room so that we reduce our levels of stress.
- ☐ Using deep breathing, mindfulness, and calming activities at the start of the exam can help.
- ☐ Remember the importance of sharing what works with your buddies.
- ☐ Asking for help from friends, family and staff is a great idea.

04

WHAT YOU WOULD TELL ALF

Think about the tips you'd suggest to Tiny Alf

ACTION – what can be done to help in exams?

LEARN – what can you share that you've learned from past stress?

FEEL – how would he be feeling?

05

CHECK-IN WITH TINY 'A.L.F':

ONE **ACTION** YOU CAN TAKE:

WHAT DID YOU **LEARN**?

HOW ARE YOU **FEELING**?

TEMPLATES AND INSTRUCTIONS ARE AVAILABLE TO DOWNLOAD VIA: JOESBUDDYLINE.ORG/BUDDIESTOOLS

38

9 BULLYING - WHY AND WHAT TO DO

There are different kinds of bullying. People can hurt each other by kicking, hitting, and pushing or by name-calling, and teasing.

People can spread rumours or exclude others from the group. Some bullying is hard to see, especially with bullying on the internet. It's important for you - or anyone being bullied - to talk.

Joe and Connie are sitting on the sofa in the living room. Joe is crying and Connie puts her arm around him.

1. What's wrong Joe? Why are you crying?

2. I'm really sorry. I know I look like a wimp.

3. No you don't! You just look upset to me. But what's going on - how can I help?

4. I've been bottling it up for ages. I haven't been able to tell anyone.

HOW DO YOU FEEL WHEN YOU SEE SOMEONE CRY? HOW HAVE YOU BEEN ABLE TO HELP THEM?

9. I know. But it's not okay. He shouldn't bully other people just because he's having issues. What are you going to do about it? You have to tell someone.

10. I know. I could talk to Mrs Handon tomorrow, I just don't want Manu to get into trouble.

WHAT DO YOU THINK BULLYING FEEL LIKE?

9 BULLYING – WHY AND WHAT TO DO: PLAYTIME

5 TOP TIPS

1. Talk to someone
2. Stay calm and confident
3. Avoid the bully
4. Be strong and brave
5. Get support from a trusted person

PICTURES SAY...

We don't just communicate with our voices – our bodies can say how we feel too.

Look at some magazine pictures, photos or on social media.

What do you think the bodies are communicating? Look at faces, arms, how people stand etc.

41 GAIN A STAR AS YOU TRAVEL AROUND THE BOARD AND FINISH EACH TASK – COLOUR IT IN WHEN COMPLETED

CHECK-IN WITH TINY 'A.L.F':

ONE **ACTION** YOU CAN TAKE:

WHAT DID YOU **LEARN**?

HOW ARE YOU **FEELING**?

05

03

CREATE A POSTER

Design and make an anti-bullying poster.

Remember to include some advice, why it's wrong and how harmful it can be.

BUDDY FACTS

- Bullying takes many forms. It can be physical, emotional, or virtual i.e. on the internet or via social media.
- It's important to understand why people might bully. They may feel powerless, they may have low self-esteem — or feel left out if they don't join in the bullying.
- Sometimes people bully without realising why they're doing it. Also, some people are bullied at home and feel sad, lonely or isolated which can cause them to lash out at others and bully.
- The most important thing, if you're experiencing bullying, is to seek help. It will not stop unless you are either assertive yourself or you have adults around you that can help tackle it.
- Remember, bullying can damage you. It is most important to ask for help as quickly as possible.

MY SCRIPT

Imagine someone is bullying you and saying you're no good at something.

What would you like to say? Be calm, focused and brave.

Write down your script — and test it with a friend that you trust.

04

TEMPLATES AND INSTRUCTIONS ARE AVAILABLE TO DOWNLOAD VIA: JOESBUDDYLINE.ORG/BUDDIESTOOLS

10 CREATING A POSITIVE SELF-CARE PLAN

Self-care is about taking care of yourself and your well-being. It means doing things that make you feel good, happy and healthy.

This can include things like getting enough sleep, eating healthy food, spending time with friends and family, and doing activities that you enjoy.

Poppy and Theo are walking in the park together...

1. I'm really bored with this. It's not nice weather and I'm getting cold and wet.

2. It's not that cold, Theo. The sun has only just gone in, and we've only been here a few minutes.

DO YOU LIKE TO TAKE WALKS?

9. Well, I do like football – oh, and swimming. I can only do those once a week so I guess I need something else too, don't I?

10. Absolutely! Ms Jones said if we want to have healthy minds and bodies, we need to exercise each day. Even a quick or steady run round the block!

WHAT COULD STOP PEOPLE DOING WHAT THEY ENJOY?

43

10 CREATING A POSITIVE SELF-CARE PLAN: PLAYTIME

BEST BUDDIES
To help us with our self-care, it can be important to spend time with people we like.

Make a list of people that help you to feel good, to laugh, who you feel safe with, that encourage and support you.

01

WHAT WE TELL OURSEL[VES]
Daily affirmations – the things we can choose to s[ay] to ourselves – are really important. You need to repeat them regularly. Write a list that you can use, e.g.

I am strong.
I belong.
I have lots to be proud of[.]
I have lots of great qualiti[es.]

02

MINDFUL JOURNAL
Let's try starting a mindful journal! Here's a framework to help get started:

DATE..
TODAY, I AM FEELING................
BECAUSE..................................
WHAT I NEED RIGHT NOW IS
....
I'M TRYING TO STAY POSITIVE
BY DOING..................................

03

45 GAIN A STAR AS YOU TRAVEL AROUND THE BOARD AND FINISH EACH TASK – COLOUR IT IN WHEN COMPLETED

04

DAILY SELF-CARE PLAN

- My morning self-care routine...
- My activity self-care routine...
- My healthy habits for self-care
- My connection to others plan
- My mindful plan

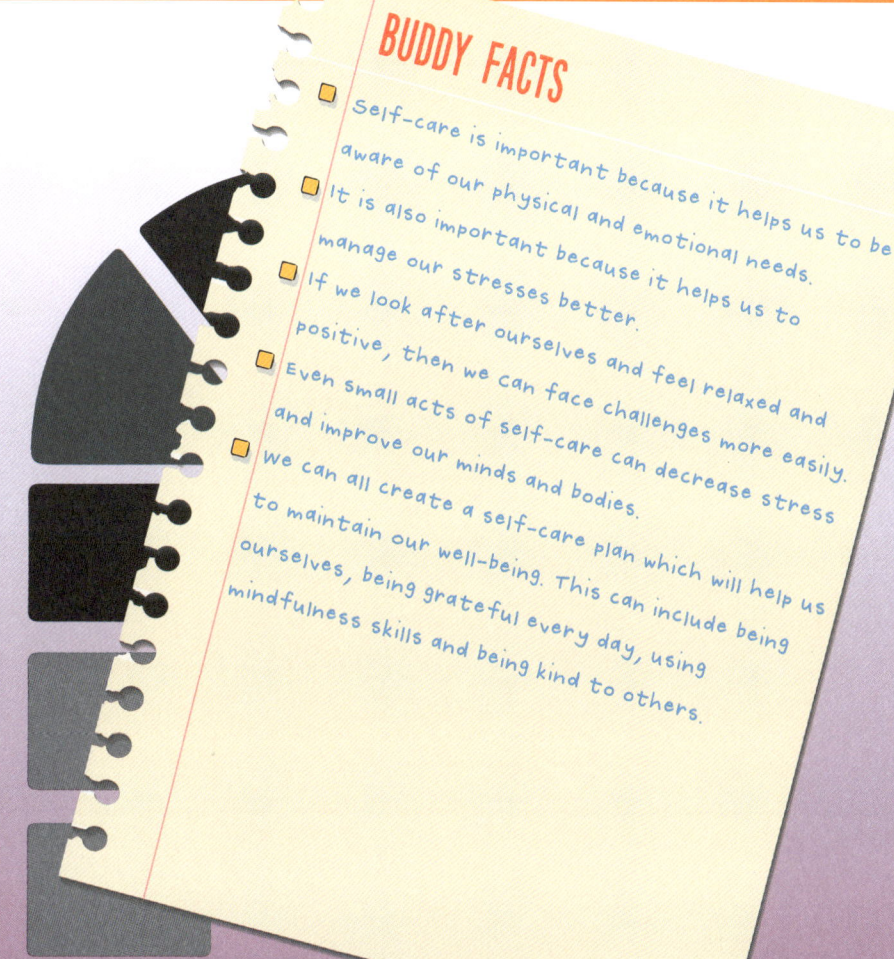

BUDDY FACTS

- Self-care is important because it helps us to be aware of our physical and emotional needs.
- It is also important because it helps us to manage our stresses better.
- If we look after ourselves and feel relaxed and positive, then we can face challenges more easily.
- Even small acts of self-care can decrease stress and improve our minds and bodies.
- We can all create a self-care plan which will help us to maintain our well-being. This can include being ourselves, being grateful every day, using mindfulness skills and being kind to others.

05

CHECK-IN WITH TINY 'A.L.F':

ONE **ACTION** YOU CAN TAKE:
_____
_____

WHAT DID YOU **LEARN**?
_____
_____

HOW ARE YOU **FEELING**?
_____
_____

TEMPLATES AND INSTRUCTIONS ARE AVAILABLE TO DOWNLOAD VIA: JOESBUDDYLINE.ORG/BUDDIESTOOLS

11 CREATING A CALM-DOWN TOOL KIT

Everyone can get upset and feel overwhelmed sometimes. This can lead us to have 'meltdown' moments when we simply feel like we can't cope and need to escape a situation.

What we really need to do is be able to calm ourselves down. Sometimes this is easier said than done. Having a 'calm down' plan is important for us so we have some strategies to help.

Joe and Annie are coming in from the playground. Annie is looking upset.

1 Hey Annie! What's up? You look red in the face.

2 I feel so angry I could burst!!!

WHEN HAVE YOU FELT LIKE ANNIE? HOW DID YOU CALM DOWN?

7 Well, you didn't! otherwise you'd have been in big trouble.

8 I know that. I feel so angry, I could just punch her!

9 No Annie! You can't do that. You know you'll get into trouble – you need to calm down.

10 I can't calm down. If she comes anywhere near me, I will get very angry with her!

HOW WOULD YOU REACT TO THIS SITUATION?

11 CREATING A CALM-DOWN TOOL KIT: PLAYTIME

01

OUR SENSES

What senses can you use to help stay calm? Here are some examples.

- ☐ Cuddle a soft blanket
- ☐ Smell the fresh air outside
- ☐ Feel the shower on your skin
- ☐ Lie down somewhere safely and listen to music
- ☐ Stroke a friendly pet

02

BELLY BREATHING

Place your hand on your belly.

Take in a short deep breath.

Watch your belly rise with you hand on it as you breathe out.

Repeat this process for a few minutes while paying attention.

03

CALM DOWN KIT

- ☐ Mix glue and hot water
- ☐ Add some food colouring
- ☐ Whisk until the mixture 'melts'
- ☐ Add glitter - and mix again
- ☐ Pour into an empty jar
- ☐ Top up with water until full
- ☐ Let it cool down
- ☐ Secure the lid
- ☐ Shake and watch the glitter when you need to calm yourself

49 GAIN A STAR AS YOU TRAVEL AROUND THE BOARD AND FINISH EACH TASK - COLOUR IT IN WHEN COMPLETED

05

CHECK-IN WITH TINY 'A.L.F':

ONE **ACTION** YOU CAN TAKE:
_____

WHAT DID YOU **LEARN**?
_____

HOW ARE YOU **FEELING**?
_____

IMAGINE!

Close your eyes.
Picture yourself gathering your feelings.
Scrunch them up.
Put them in a box and close it.
Put the box away.

Now still imagining...
walk, run, or skip away
from the painful feelings.

04

BUDDY FACTS

- Self-regulation is the ability to manage your emotions and behaviour during situations. It includes being able to resist highly emotional reactions to upsetting events or situations, to calm yourself down when you get upset, to adjust, and to handle frustrations.

- It is a set of skills that enable us to direct our own behaviour towards a goal, despite things being uncertain around us. It is the ability to:
  - ☐ Recognise and manage emotions
  - ☐ Control impulses
  - ☐ Enjoy looking forward to achieving good outcomes
  - ☐ Make thoughtful and conscious choices
  - ☐ And set goals and achieve them

- If we can keep calm and self-regulated we can then listen to our inner voice to make better decisions. We won't feel overwhelmed and will be able to focus and maintain more positive relationships.

TEMPLATES AND INSTRUCTIONS ARE AVAILABLE TO DOWNLOAD VIA: JOESBUDDYLINE.ORG/BUDDIESTOOLS

12 LEARNING TO CONTROL YOUR MIND

Go

We know that being in nature helps us because it gives us a break from being busy every day, it lowers our stress levels and helps us top up on vitamin D. This is the vitamin that releases serotonin in our brains – one of the good chemicals.

Learning to be mindful helps too. This means we pay attention to the 'here and now' – the present – rather than worrying about what has happened or might happen in the future.

Alex and Ella are about to leave school for the day and are stood at the school gates chatting.

7 I suppose you're right I just found it so difficult to stop thoughts racing through my head.

8 I get it – but it's like riding a bike. You'll only get better if you keep trying. It's really helpful and will help you be calmer.

9 Perhaps it's just not something I can do, Ella.

10 I don't think you'll know until you really try. It definitely helped me to know how to focus on my work. I did really well with my English writing afterwards.

WHAT THOUGHTS CAN FILL YOUR MIND? HOW HAVE YOU BEEN ABLE TO MAKE THEM POSITIVE?

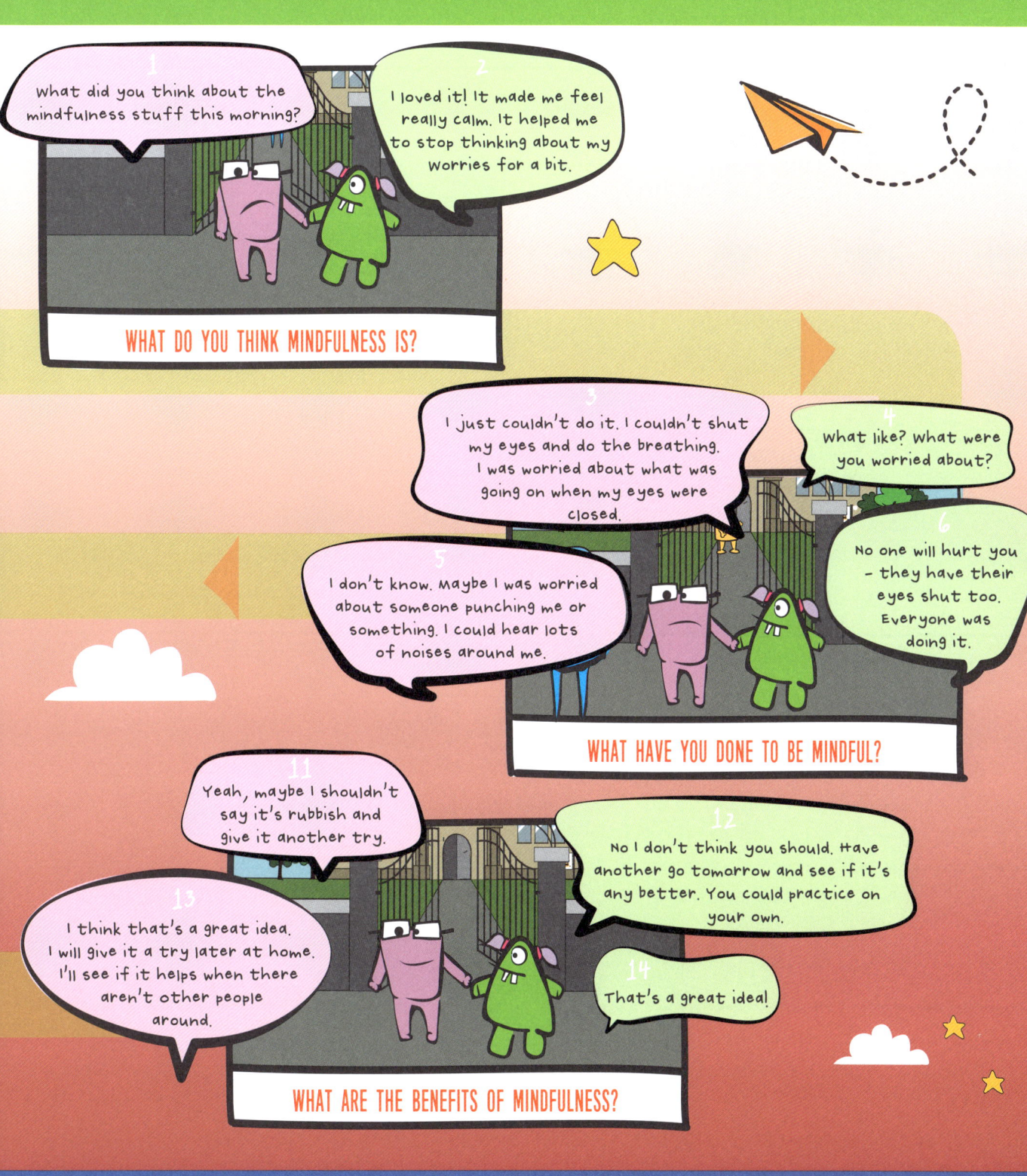

12 LEARNING TO CONTROL YOUR MIND: PLAYTIME

01

GROUNDING

Stand thinking about how you feel right now. Now look around you to find...

- **5** Things you can see
- **4** Things you can hear
- **3** Things you can feel
- **2** Things you can smell
- **1** Big slow short breath

02

WALK IN NATURE

Take a walk outside.
What can you notice?
Say each thing in your head.
How do you feel?
What can you smell?
What can you hear?

03

EXERCISE DIARY

Keep a diary with the following:

DAY

EXERCISE

HOW I FELT BEFORE

HOW I FELT AFTER

GAIN A STAR AS YOU TRAVEL AROUND THE BOARD AND FINISH EACH TASK - COLOUR IT IN WHEN COMPLETED

04 BODY SCAN

Sit on a chair or the floor.

Close your eyes.

Starting at your toes, think about each part of your body in turn.

Try and relax it before you move to the next part.

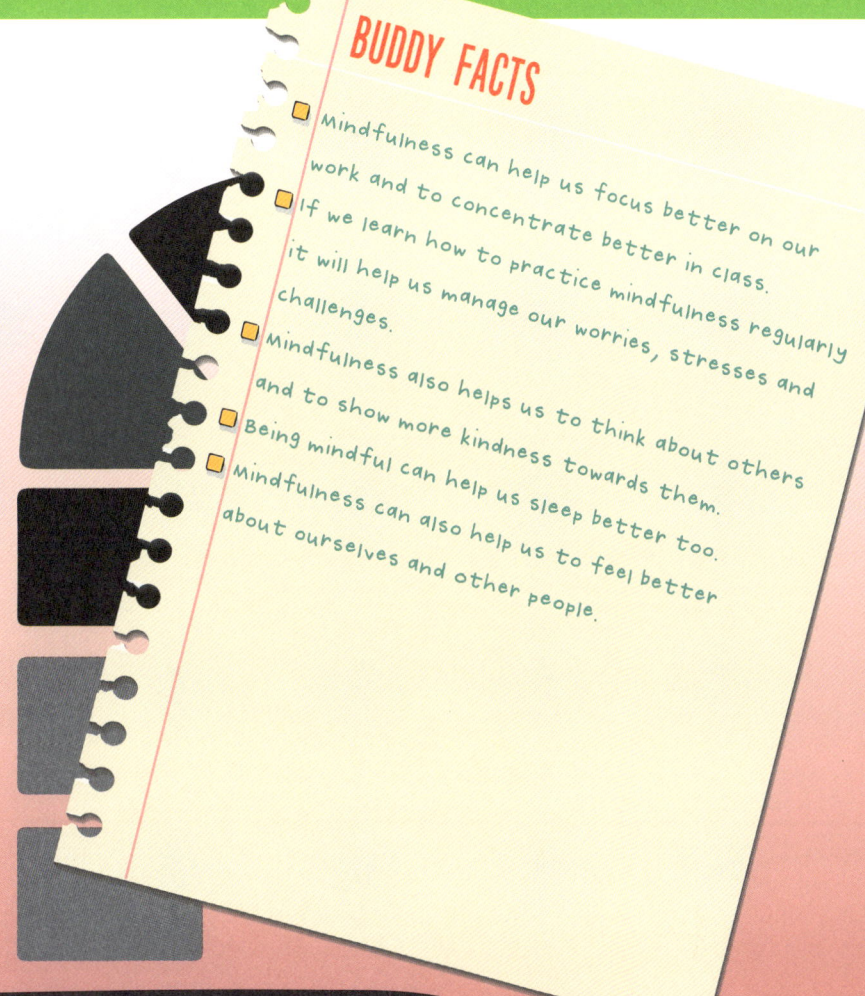

BUDDY FACTS

- Mindfulness can help us focus better on our work and to concentrate better in class.
- If we learn how to practice mindfulness regularly it will help us manage our worries, stresses and challenges.
- Mindfulness also helps us to think about others and to show more kindness towards them.
- Being mindful can help us sleep better too.
- Mindfulness can also help us to feel better about ourselves and other people.

05

CHECK-IN WITH TINY 'A.L.F':

ONE **ACTION** YOU CAN TAKE:

WHAT DID YOU **LEARN**?

HOW ARE YOU **FEELING**?

TEMPLATES AND INSTRUCTIONS ARE AVAILABLE TO DOWNLOAD VIA: JOESBUDDYLINE.ORG/BUDDIESTOOLS

13 USING KINDNESS AND GRATITUDE

Positive psychology is the study of what makes human-beings happier, healthy and to be at our best.

It's not possible to be happy all the time. Sometimes we feel sad, worried or anxious. To help with this, being kind to ourselves and others is really important.

Poppy and Joe are planning their 'kindness week'. Joe is writing and Poppy is next to him.

7 Love that! But maybe we should say 'no' to presents because people can't afford it. We could just stick with the cards. They are a lovely thing.

8 Okay yeah, great thought. Then everyone can do an act of kindness with no problem. What about Thursday or Friday then?

WHO DO YOU KNOW THAT SHOWS KINDNESS?

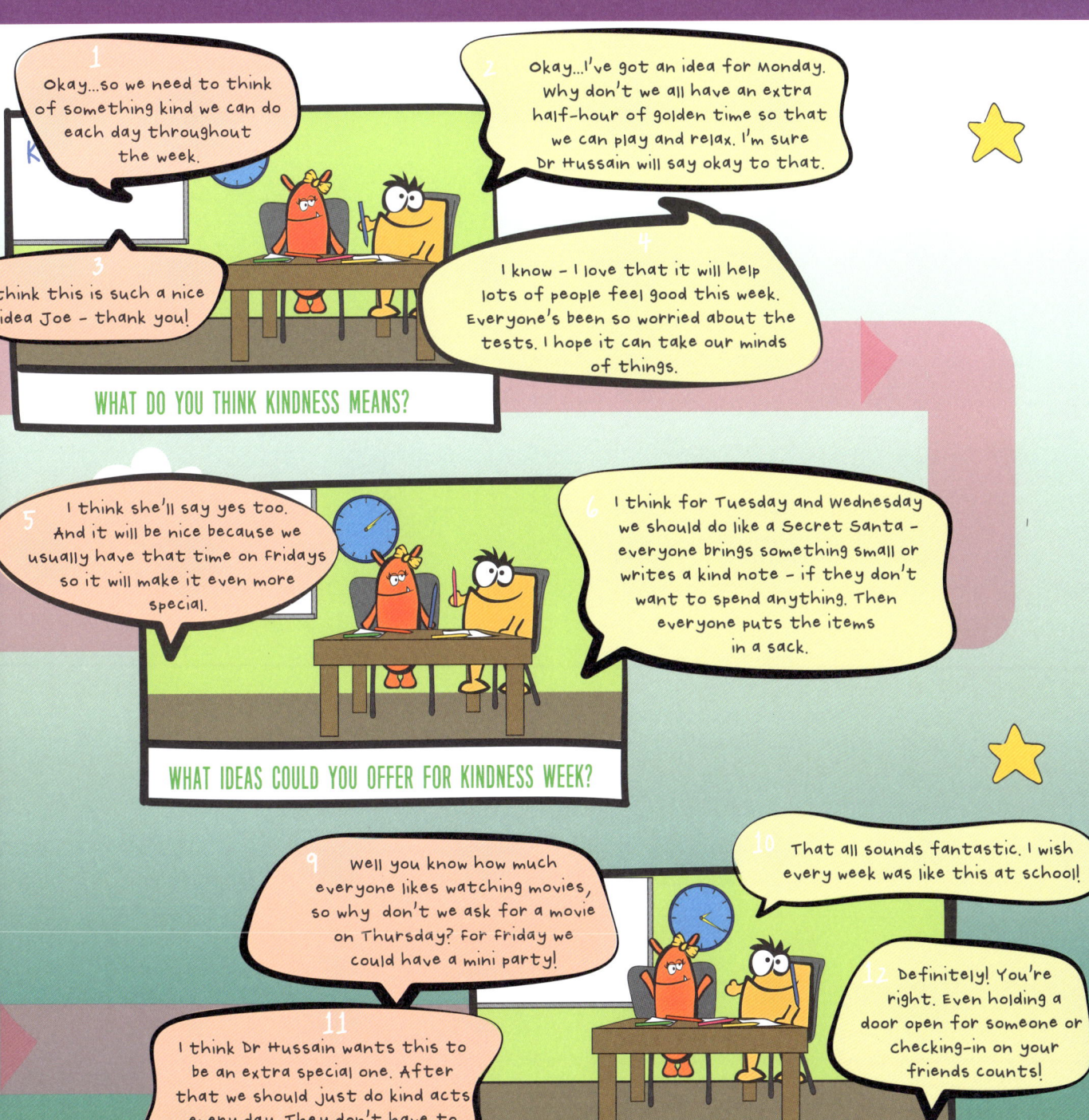

13 USING KINDNESS AND GRATITUDE: PLAYTIME

01

POSITIVE DIARY

Keep a daily note of...

Best 3 things that happened.
3 people you're grateful for.
What you're most proud of.
What you did that was kind.
Score for the day (10 is best).

03

GRATITUDE JAR

Try and write something you're grateful for each day on a small piece of paper and keep it in a jar.

02

DAILY KINDNESS

Keep a note of anything kind that you do each day and what kindness other people have shown you each day.

57 GAIN A STAR AS YOU TRAVEL AROUND THE BOARD AND FINISH EACH TASK - COLOUR IT IN WHEN COMPLETED

04

LETTER TO MY BUDDY

Write a letter - or short note - to your buddy, best friend or someone you care about.

Tell them what you like most about them and what you appreciate about them.

To Will,

BUDDY FACTS

- We can all feel happier every day if we focus on the positives about ourselves and others.
- Feeling grateful every day for what we have and what we're doing builds our well-being.
- Doing kind things for other people also increases feelings of happiness and well-being.
- Acts of kindness – and choosing to think kindly – makes everyone feel better as well as making the world a better place.
- To help kindness and gratitude, it will help to find good Buddies not bad friends.

05

CHECK-IN WITH TINY 'A.L.F':

ONE **ACTION** YOU CAN TAKE:

WHAT DID YOU **LEARN**?

HOW ARE YOU **FEELING**?

TEMPLATES AND INSTRUCTIONS ARE AVAILABLE TO DOWNLOAD VIA: JOESBUDDYLINE.ORG/BUDDIESTOOLS

14 USING YOUR WORRIES WELL

GO

Everyone worries sometimes. This is a normal part of being a human-being.

The important thing is to remember that we should not be worried for most of the time as this means we will not be able to do all the things we should - or want to - do including playing with friends and relaxing.

Annie and Arti are walking round the playground together. They sit on a Buddy Bench to have a quiet chat.

7. Well when I get home from school, I write down everything I'm worried about and leave it in the kitchen. When my mum gets home from work we sit together and read it.

8. How does that help?

9. When we talk it through my mum tries to help me to see I don't need to worry about some things. For the things that are worrying, we work out a plan to help.

10. But what about when things worry you at school?

WHO DO YOU - OR COULD YOU - SHARE YOUR WORRIES WITH?

11. I've got a 'worry book'. I write down things as they worry me and then add them to my list after school - so I can talk to my mum about them later.

12. But that means you've still got the worry inside you all day.

CAN YOU DRAW WHAT YOU'RE WORRIED ABOUT?

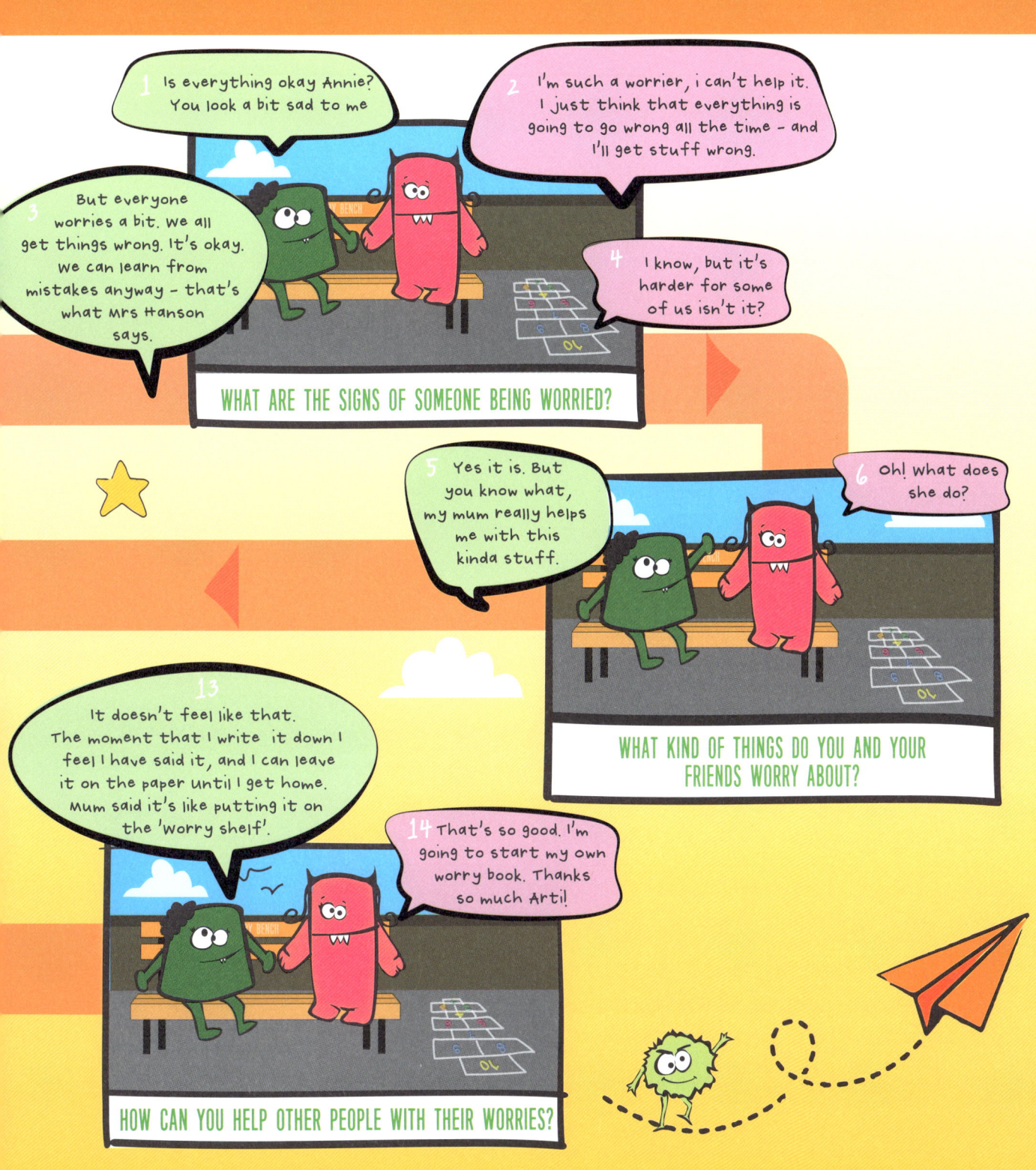

14 USING YOUR WORRIES WELL: PLAYTIME

WORRY TIME

Choose a time of day for your "worry time" - and how long you will 'worry' for. Draw it on the clock by shading the time (from - to). Practice using just this time to think about your worries.

WORK THE WORRY

Write down your biggest worry...

When do you worry most about it?
Where are you when you feel worried about it?
What could you do differently?
What would help to reduce your worry?

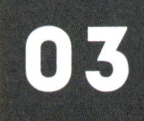

WORRY PLACE

Now you have your time (and how long you will worry), you can think of a place to worry.
It could be in the garden, for example.
Where do you feel safe?

You can even tell the plants, birds or trees your worries!

61 GAIN A STAR AS YOU TRAVEL AROUND THE BOARD AND FINISH EACH TASK - COLOUR IT IN WHEN COMPLETED

04

BUILD A PLAN

This is your personal plan to help manage your worries.

*What makes me worry?
What makes it worse?
What helps me?
What small steps can I take?*

3 things to calm myself, activities to help my well-being, people I can talk to...

BUDDY FACTS

- Everyone gets worried sometimes. It's normal to feel this way. We can learn ways to cope with our worries in a few ways.
- Talking to a trusted person and telling them what we're worrying about is always important.
- Sometimes our worries can be pushed aside or dismissed by other people. It is important not to let this happen if you genuinely feel worried!
- If you can share it, it's easier to sort it.
- Taking time out to worry can help but we can also learn how to problem-solve with others so that we can feel and work better.

05

CHECK-IN WITH TINY 'A.L.F':

ONE **ACTION** YOU CAN TAKE:
_____
_____

WHAT DID YOU **LEARN**?
_____
_____

HOW ARE YOU **FEELING**?
_____
_____

TEMPLATES AND INSTRUCTIONS ARE AVAILABLE TO DOWNLOAD VIA: JOESBUDDYLINE.ORG/BUDDIESTOOLS

15 STAYING SAFE - INCLUDING ONLINE

Self-harm is when someone hurts themselves on purpose. This can be done in many ways - cutting, scratching or burning oneself.

It is important to know that self-harm is not a healthy way to cope with difficult situations. It can be a sign that help and support is needed. It is important to talk to someone.

Annie and Connie are in Annie's bedroom. They're looking at their phones.

1. You know, yesterday I saw something really horrible on here.
2. What?!
3. It was someone cutting their arms.
4. Really? Why would they do that?

WHAT DO YOU THINK ABOUT SELF-HARM?

9. Did you talk to your mum about that, Connie?
10. No, I didn't. I just wouldn't want to worry her.
11. I think you should. I think she'd be more worried if you didn't say anything.
12. You really think so?

WHAT DO YOU THINK CONNIE SHOULD DO?

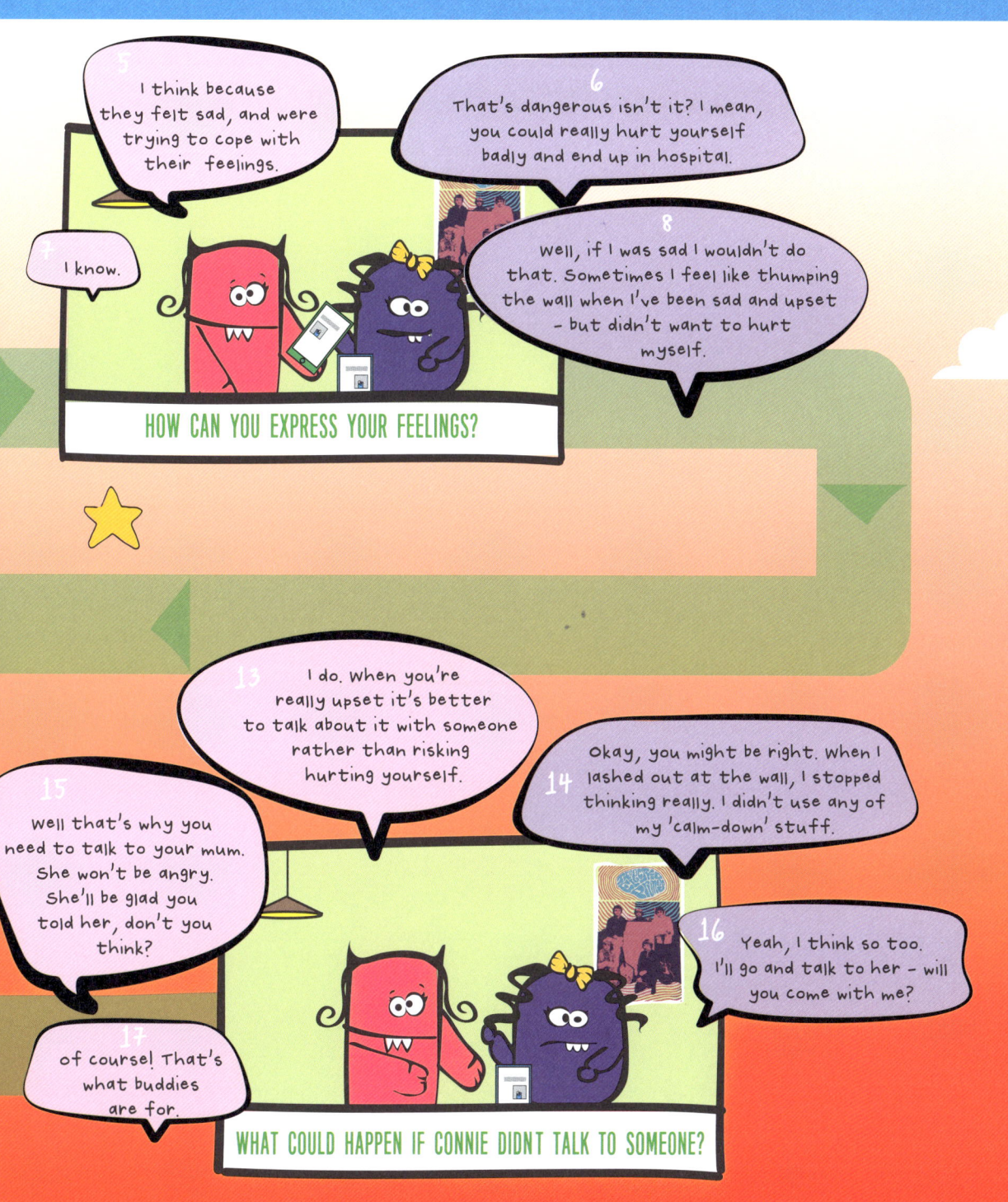

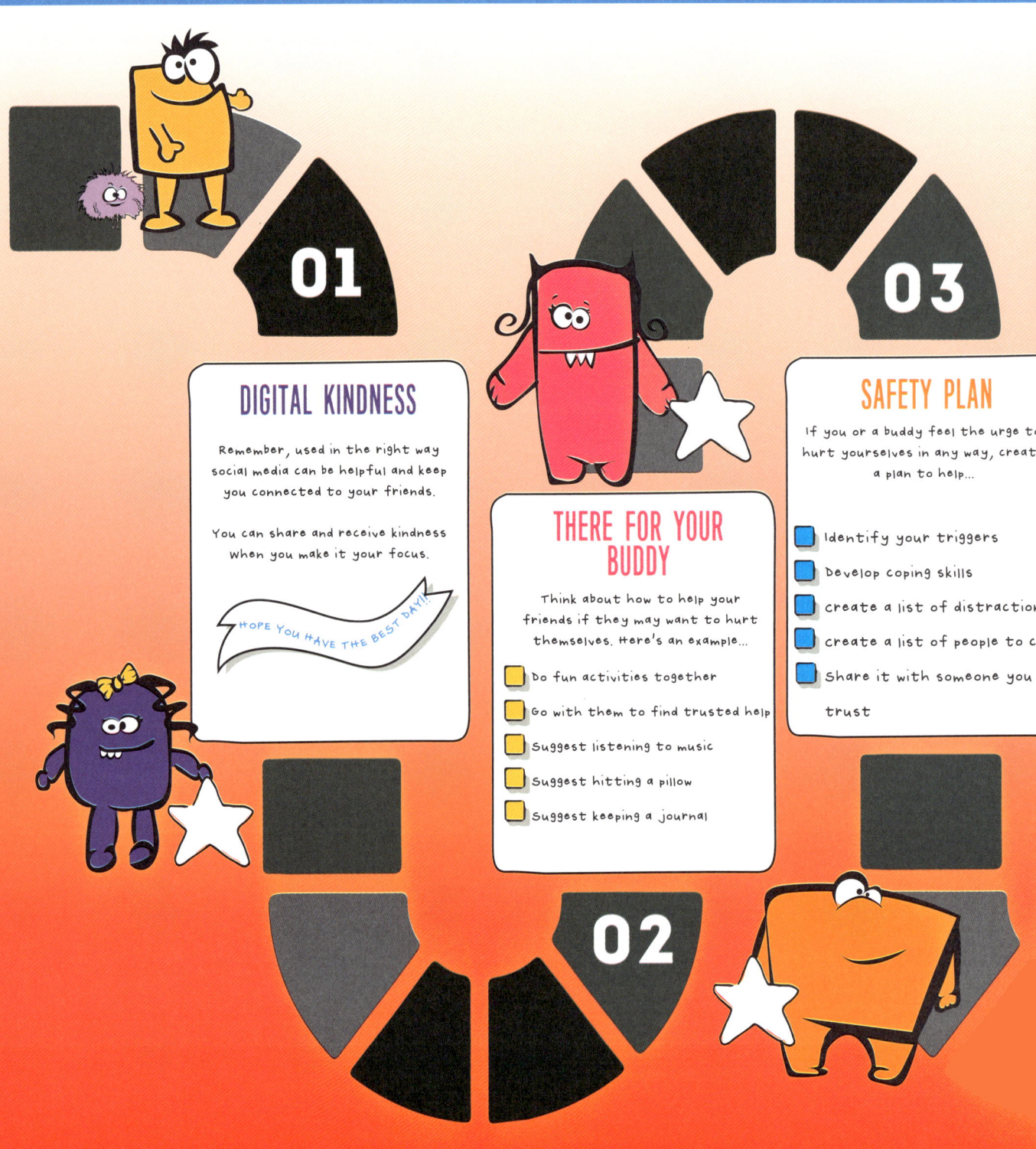

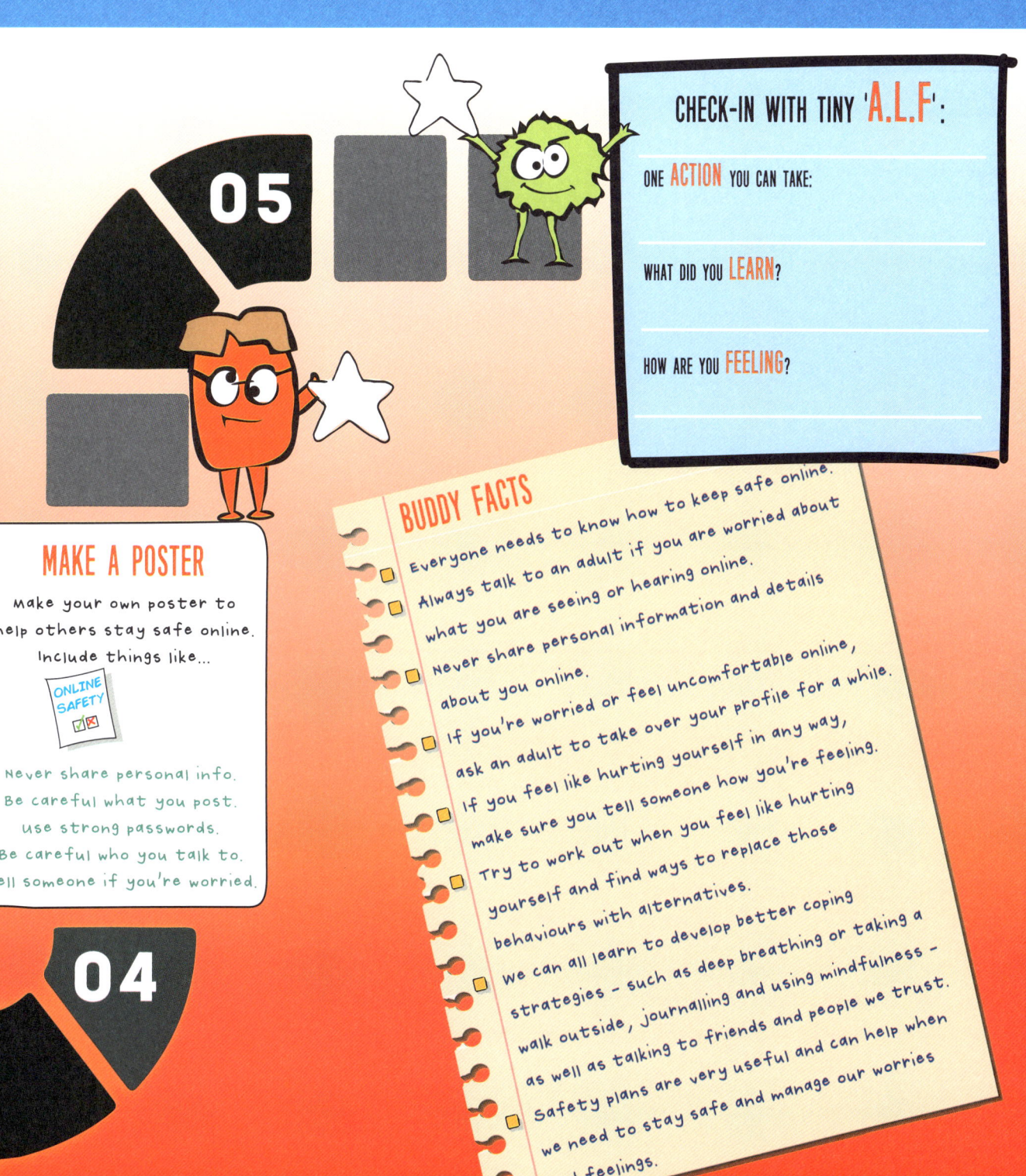

16 CREATING YOUR OWN BUDDIES PLAN

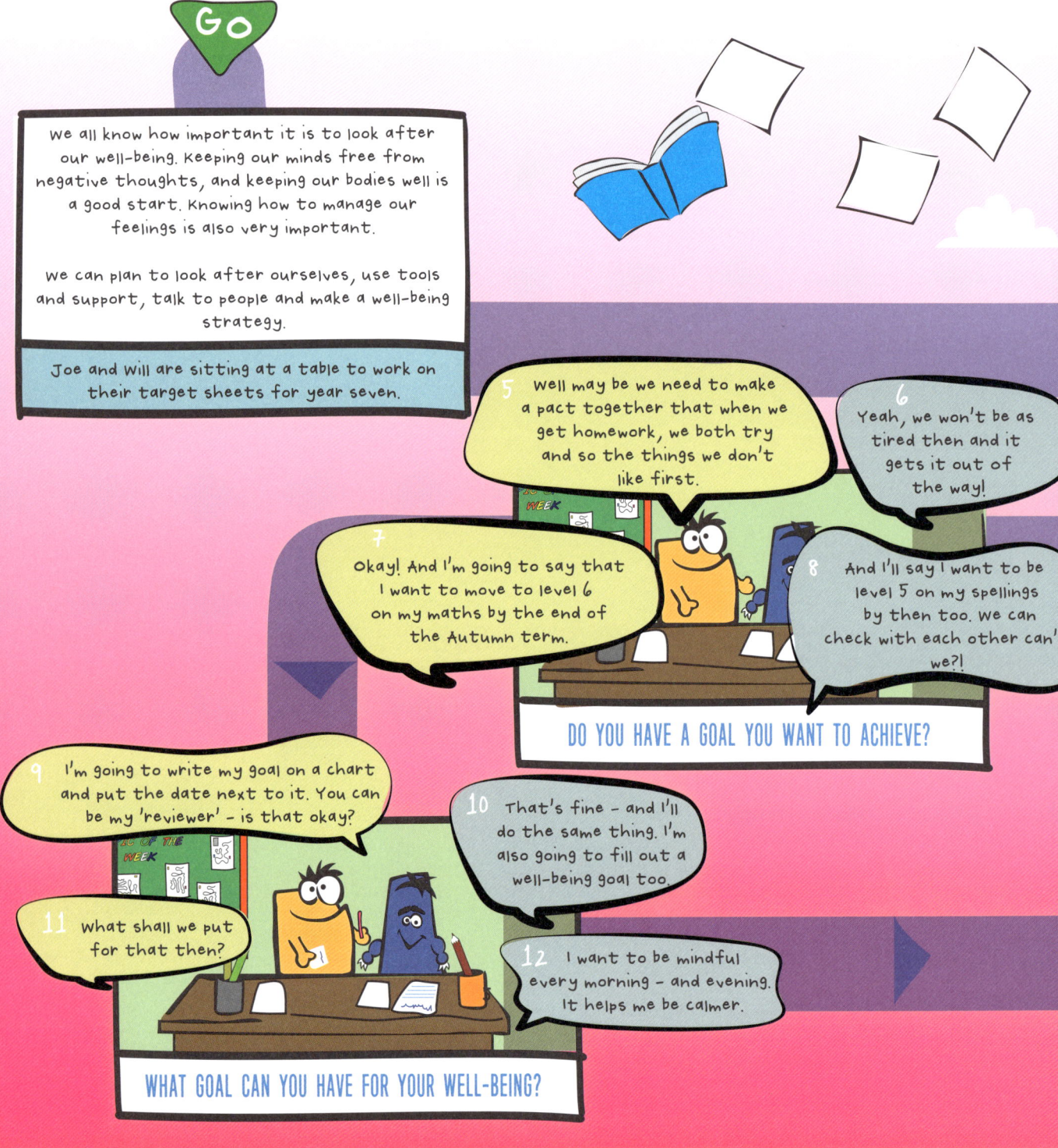

We all know how important it is to look after our well-being. Keeping our minds free from negative thoughts, and keeping our bodies well is a good start. Knowing how to manage our feelings is also very important.

We can plan to look after ourselves, use tools and support, talk to people and make a well-being strategy.

Joe and Will are sitting at a table to work on their target sheets for year seven.

5. Well maybe we need to make a pact together that when we get homework, we both try and do the things we don't like first.

6. Yeah, we won't be as tired then and it gets it out of the way!

7. Okay! And I'm going to say that I want to move to level 6 on my maths by the end of the Autumn term.

8. And I'll say I want to be level 5 on my spellings by then too. We can check with each other can't we?!

DO YOU HAVE A GOAL YOU WANT TO ACHIEVE?

9. I'm going to write my goal on a chart and put the date next to it. You can be my 'reviewer' - is that okay?

10. That's fine - and I'll do the same thing. I'm also going to fill out a well-being goal too.

11. What shall we put for that then?

12. I want to be mindful every morning - and evening. It helps me be calmer.

WHAT GOAL CAN YOU HAVE FOR YOUR WELL-BEING?

16 CREATING YOUR OWN 'BUDDIES' PLAN: PLAYTIME

TREE OF CONFIDENCE

Draw a tree with lots of branches. On each branch write the name of people that give you confidence.

Add leaves to your tree. In each one write words to describe the characteristics that help build your confidence e.g. brave, kind etc.

MY POSITIVE SCROLL

Design and make your personal scroll full of positive thoughts.

Use your favourite colours. Keep it somewhere you can see.

PERSONAL PLAN

Create your 'Personal Positive Activities Plan'.
In your plan, write down each item and include:

- ☑ What you'll do
- ☑ When you'll do it (day/time)
- ☑ How much time you'll spend on it
- ☑ What you want to achieve

69 GAIN A STAR AS YOU TRAVEL AROUND THE BOARD AND FINISH EACH TASK - COLOUR IT IN WHEN COMPLETED

MEET THE PEOPLE BEHIND THE BOOK

Hello. I'm **Dr Tina Rae**, the author of this book. I really enjoyed writing it and working with Dani who has made everything look so beautiful! I hope that you have enjoyed working through all the activities and reading the stories. I also hope that you have learnt lots of new strategies to try out and have taken away the key message that it is **always good to talk** about how we feel and think about ourselves and the world that we live in. I have written over 100 books now, but am probably the proudest of this one as it really means so much to me to be able to share my ideas and know that they may make a big difference to so many children and young people.

As a writer, psychologist, teacher and artist I have always worked with children and young people. I have learnt that all of us have times when we are sad, anxious and worried about things. I have also learnt that there is a lot that we can do to help ourselves and also to help our friends and those that we love. I call myself a Positive Psychologist. This is because I look for strengths and what helps people to be happier and lead healthier and more meaningful lives. We can all learn to use our strengths to improve our well-being. We can also all learn how to share our worries and manage them more effectively. The way to do this is to talk, share our concerns and share our ideas and ways of coping. I hope that this book will help you to do just that.

Dr Tina

Hi there, I'm **Dani** (pronounced DAY-NEE) **Saveker**. The design of the book and the creation of the Buddies' world and characters was my job. When I first saw Dr Tina's words I wondered how I could bring it all to life and create something fun and interesting for you and your teachers. Creating the Buddies' world reminded me of the work I've done for my own mental health - from childhood through to being a busy and successful business leader and mum to my three children. We all need to remember how important it is to talk - and work on our minds and bodies!

The changing world around us can be frightening, fast-paced and challenging at times, but it is also full of adventures and opportunities. We just need to learn how to navigate the tough stuff and keep moving forwards. I truly hope that this book - and all that comes from it - will be something you'll enjoy reading, using and having in your life. I believe that tackling difficult subjects and being able to talk about them can also be creative and fun. Let your imagination go to work and remember that sharing your feelings is really brave. I hope you love the characters as much as I did in creating them for you. You can always let me know what you think of them by emailing me: **dani@danisaveker.com**.

Dani

ABOUT JOES BUDDY LINE

At the age of just 31, in August 2020, we lost our beloved Joe. A caring son, brother, a wonderful friend and a talented, award-winning Radio Producer. He brought a cheeky spirit and constant laughter to all those that met him. His selflessness and commitment to helping others touched so many, and we are dedicated to carrying this on for him. Set up in the memory and legacy of Joe Lyons, Joe's Buddy Line is a Registered Charity within England and Wales.

We aim to provide emotional and mental health initiatives and support for stakeholders within and around Primary School to University, by offering workshops run by certified mental health practitioners - in addition to tools, ways to open up conversations and range of approaches.

Your mental health is as important as your physical health and we must fight to encourage everyone to know that they are not alone, starting with students.

Contact details:

Web: joesbuddyline.org

General enquiries: info@joesbuddyline.org

www.instagram.com/joesbuddyline/

If you need support text: **joesbuddy** to 85258 for a conversation with a trained SHOUT volunteer 24/7

Registered Charity Number 1193127

If you are over 18 years of age, willing and able to donate to Joe's Buddy Line you would be helping us to continue assisting more schools - within our Approved Area of Charitable Objectives in England and Wales. Schools ask for our help with initiatives and workshops for students and, where also possible, for all within their school families.

Please go to: www.joesbuddyline.org and click the DONATE button. If you are also able to sign the necessary declaration, please tick the Gift Aid option. This will then allow additional funding to go to the Charity with no further cost to you. Thank you very much for any support that can be given to us.

USEFUL RESOURCES

Action for Children
actionforchildren.org.uk
Charity supporting children, young people, and their families across England.

Anxiety UK
03444 775 774 (helpline)
07537 416 905 (text)
anxietyuk.org.uk
Advice and support for people living with anxiety.

Beat
0808 801 0711 (youthline)
0808 801 0811 (studentline)
beateatingdisorders.co.uk
Under 18s helpline, webchat and online support groups for people with eating disorders, such as anorexia and bulimia.

Childline
0800 1111
childline.org.uk
Support for children and young people in the UK, including a free 24-hour helpline.

Hope Again
0808 808 1677
hopeagain.org.uk
Support for young people when someone dies.

Kooth
kooth.com
Counsellors available until 10pm every day. Free, safe, and anonymous online counselling for young people.

Me and My Mind
meandmymind.nhs.uk
Advice and support for young people struggling with unusual experiences, such as hearing voices.

Mencap
0808 808 1111
mencap.org.uk
Information and advice for people with a learning disability, families, and carers.

Mind
Infoline: 0300 123 3393
Mind.org.uk
Offering advice and information to people with mental health problems

National Society for the Prevention of Cruelty to Children (NSPCC)
0800 800 5000
0800 1111 (18 or under)
nspcc.org.uk
Support for children and anyone worried about a child.

OCD Youth
ocdyouth.org
Youth Support for young people with obsessive-compulsive disorder (OCD).

On My Mind
annafreud.org/on-my-mind
Information for young people to make informed choices about their mental health and well-being.

Place 2 Be
General enquiries: 020 7923 5500
Place2be.org.uk
A children and young people's mental health charity working with pupils, families and staff in UK schools

Samaritans
116 123
samaritans.org
Freepost RSRB-KKBY-CYJK
PO Box 90 90
Stirling FK8 2SA
jo@samaritans.org
24-hour emotional support for anyone who needs to talk.

Shout
Text: Shout to 85258
giveusashout.org
A free confidential 24/7 text messaging service for anyone in the UK who needs support

The Mix
0808 808 4994
85258 (crisis messenger service, Text THEMIX)
themix.org.uk
Support and advice for under 25s, including webchat.

YoungMinds
0808 802 5544 (parents helpline)
85258 (crisis messenger service, text YM)
youngminds.org.uk
Committed to improving the mental health of babies, children and young people, including support for parents and carers.

COPYRIGHT AND OTHER IMPORTANT INFORMATION

First published in 2024 by Joe's Buddy Line Charity.
Registered Charity (no. 1193127) in England and Wales.

Author Copyright ©Tina Rae, 2024.
Illustrations, Typeset and Design Copyright ©Dani Saveker 2024.
Foreword Copyright ©Roman Kemp, 2024.
Published by Joe's Buddy Line Charity.
Distributed by Joe's Buddy Line Charity.
All Rights Reserved.
Printed and bound by Dyer and Son Ltd, 32 North St, Leatherhead, Surrey KT22 7AT in Great Britain.

The moral rights of the Author, Designer and Illustrator have been asserted.
No part of the Buddies Talk book may be reproduced, distributed or transmitted without the prior written permission of Joe's Buddy Line Charity.

The Buddies Talk book is intended to help open up conversations with the aim that mental health becomes as normal to talk about as physical health, and to support educational settings within England and Wales, in the important work they do towards the well-being of students, teachers and others within their communities. Neither Joe's Buddy Line Charity, the Author, nor the Designer/ Illustrator are responsible for the content of any websites, or any contact information, that may be mentioned.

Any perceived slight of any individual or organisation by image, drawing, description or in any other way is purely coincidental and unintentional. The resources in The Buddies Talk book are provided for informational purposes only and should not be used to replace the specialised training and professional judgment of a health care or mental health care practitioner.

If you or someone else requires specific advice and/or information or has a mental health or other concern or issue, they should consult a GP, or a suitably qualified practitioner or organisation, as soon as possible. If more immediate urgent help or assistance is required, they should attend - with, if necessary, the help of a reliable family member, friend or other trusted person - an Accident and Emergency Hospital service or call an Emergency Telephone Number (UK - 999).

Neither Joe's Buddy Line Charity, the Author, nor the Designer/ Illustrator assume any responsibility (and hereby disclaim any liability to any party for) any loss, damage, or disruption, that is incurred as a result of the use of information contained in the Buddies Talk book, including, but not limited to, any errors, omissions or misstatements.

A Cataloguing in Publication (CIP) record for this book is available from the
British Library ISBN -978-1-7385799-9- 0
https://joesbuddyline.org/

INDEX

anger, angry	12, 22, 46-48, 64	positive thinking	26, 30
anxiety	15, 17-18, 22, 30	prepare	37
appearance	32		
ask for help	10, 15, 24, 35, 42	reflect	09
		relax, relaxation	26-30, 46, 54, 56, 59
body image	31, 34		
breathing	17, 33, 38, 48-49, 52, 66, 68	sad	11, 14, 22, 35, 42, 57, 60, 64
bully, bullying	39, 41, 42	self-care	43-45, 47
		self-harm	63, 65
calm	28-29, 30, 37, 41-42, 47-52, 62, 64, 67	self-talk	25
change	09, 10, 32	strategy	67
coping	09, 35, 37, 65-66	stress	10, 16, 18, 22, 28, 30, 35, 37-38, 51, 54
creative	17	struggle	08, 10, 23, 24
cry, crying	39-40		
		tests	21, 35-38, 56
developing mind	23, 26	thinking	19, 21-22, 26, 30, 53, 64
disappoint	27	thoughts	17, 19, 21-22, 25-26, 37, 51, 67, 69
emotions	11, 13-14, 26, 42, 46, 50	transition	07-10
exams	20, 35-38		
excitement	25	vision	25
exercise	34, 43-44, 53	visualise	37
fears	14	what if…	07, 09, 36
feelings	11, 13-14, 19, 22, 25, 34, 50, 58, 64, 66-67	worry, worrying	07-08, 22, 27, 32, 35-36, 51, 58-59, 61-63, 70
gratitude	55, 57-58, 70		

MNEMONICS

ACT   26
Action - Calm - Think

ALF   each chapter 'Playtime'
Action - Learn - Feel

PMA   21
Positive Mental Attitude

SMART   70
Specific - Measure - Achieve - Relevant - Time

TFD   21
Think - Feel - Do

happy	27, 30, 34, 37, 43, 55
kindness	18, 54-58, 65, 70
looking forward	07, 08, 50
mindful, mindfulness	38, 45-46, 52, 54, 66-67, 70
negative thoughts	21-22, 67
online safety	63-66

My Progress Sheet 👍

Me as a Buddy

01. Making Your Transition Work for You
02. Understanding Your Feelings
03. Anxiety and When To Ask for Help
04. Knowing Feelings Are Not Facts
05. Developing Your Mind
06. Building Your Plan To Relax
07. Valuing Your Body and What It Can Do
08. Coping With Tests and Exams
09. Bullying - Why And What To Do
10. Creating A Positive Self-care Plan
11. Creating A Calm-down Tool Kit
12. Learning To Control Your Mind
13. Using Kindness and Gratitude
14. Using Your Worries Well
15. Staying Safe - Including online
16. Creating Your Own 'Buddies' Plan